Learn to Cook
CHINESE

Nita Mehta

B.Sc. (Home Science), M.Sc. (Food and Nutrition) Gold Medalist

Tanya Mehta

Learn to Cook
CHINESE

© Copyright 2006-2008  **SNAB** Publishers Pvt Ltd

WORLD RIGHTS RESERVED. The contents—all recipes, photographs and drawings are original and copyrighted. No portion of this book shall be reproduced, stored in a retrieval system or transmitted by any means, electronic, mechanical, photocopying, recording or otherwise, without the written permission of the publishers.

While every precaution is taken in the preparation of this book, the publisher and the author assume no responsibility for errors or omissions. Neither is any liability assumed for damages resulting from the use of information contained herein.

TRADEMARKS ACKNOWLEDGED. Trademarks used, if any, are acknowledged as trademarks of their respective owners. These are used as reference only and no trademark infringement is intended upon. Ajinomoto (monosodium glutamate, MSG) is a trademark of Aji-no-moto company of Japan. Use it sparingly if you must as a flavour enhancer.

Reprint 2008
ISBN 978-81-7869-098-8

Food Styling and Photography: **SNAB**

Layout and Laser Typesetting :

National Information Technology Academy
3A/3, Asaf Ali Road
New Delhi-110002
☎ 23252948

Published by :

Publishers Pvt. Ltd.
3A/3 Asaf Ali Road,
New Delhi - 110002
Tel: 23252948, 23250091
Telefax: 91-11-23250091

Editorial and Marketing office:
E-159, Greater Kailash-II, N.Delhi-48
Fax: 91-11-29225218, 29229558
Tel: 91-11-29214011, 29218574
E-Mail: nitamehta@email.com
nitamehta@nitamehta.com
Website: http://www.nitamehta.com
Website: http://www.snabindia.com

Contributing Writers :
Anurag Mehta
Subhash Mehta

Editorial & Proofreading :
Rakesh
Ramesh

Distributed by :

THE VARIETY BOOK DEPOT
A.V.G. Bhavan, M 3 Con Circus,
New Delhi - 110 001
Tel : 23417175, 23412567; Fax : 23415335
Email: varietybookdepot@rediffmail.com

Printed by :

CANARA TRADERS & PRINTERS PVT. LTD.,
CHENNAI

Rs. 129/-

Introduction

"Learn to Cook Chinese" will free you from all the fears you get when you plan to serve a Chinese meal. You can now cook Chinese all the way - Soups, Starters, Main Course and Desserts.

I remember serving many years back just noodles and Sweet 'n' Sour with an Indian meal. No more mixing cuisines! The book gives you the confidence to offer a splendid Chinese spread through recipes which are clearly worded with step by step instructions. The final picture makes you even more confident of the recipes.

Chinese food is full of flavour and the texture of vegetables in every dish is crisp. Keeping this in mind, the recipes have been put down in a very orderly manner, so as to retain the colour and crispiness of vegetables. The correct cutting of vegetables which exposes the maximum surface area of the vegetable, helps make cooking faster, which in turn keeps the vegetable crunchy. A special chapter on techniques of vegetable cutting and cooking is thus included.

Enjoy the taste of China, all cooked in a simple delicious manner.

CONT

Introduction   3
Chinese Ingredients and Sauces   6
About Noodles and Rice   12
Chinese Cooking Utensils   14
Chinese Cooking Methods   16
Vegetable Cutting Methods   19
Simple Vegetable Garnishes   22
Clear your doubts...   24

Soups   28

Quick Vegetable Stock   30
Fresh Vegetable Stock   30
Sweet Corn Vegetable Soup   31
Hot & Sour Soup   32
Wonton Soup   34
Talomein Soup   36
Mushroom Crispy Rice Soup   37

Starters   38

Tips for Handling Starters   39
Kimchi Salad   40
Spring Rolls   41
Shredded Potatoes   44
Steamed Momos   47
Lotus Wings   50

Accompaniments to Starters and Soups...   53

Hot & Sour Sauce   53
Sizchuan Sauce   53
Green Chillies in Vinegar   53
Sweet & Sour Sauce   53
Red Sesame Dip   54
Sweet Chilli Dip   54

Chinese Saucy Dishes 55

Potato Strings in Ginger Sauce   56
Vegetable Manchurian   58
Tofu in Hot Garlic Sauce   61
Veggies in Szechwan Sauce   64

American Chopsuey with Vegetables   67
Crispy Noodles   67
Cauliflower in Pepper Sauce   71

Chinese Stir Fries 73

Spicy Honey Veggies   74
Babycorn Aniseed   77

Hoisin Stir Fry Okra   80
Stir fried Snow Peas/Beans   83

Noodles & Rice 86

Perfect Boiled Noodles   87
Chinese Steamed Rice   87
Perfect Boiled Rice   88
Chilli Garlic Noodles   89

Haka Noodles with Vegetables   90
Glutinous Rice   92
Vegetable Chow Mein   94
Vegetable Fried Rice   96

Desserts 97

Toffee Apples   97

Glossary of Names/Terms 99

International Conversion Guide 102

Chinese Ingredients and Sauces

Before actual cooking, check if you have all the necessary sauces and seasonings. There are several items that are important in Chinese cooking, e.g. soya sauce, vinegar, cornflour etc. These essentials will help you create authentic flavours. Start with a few basic items.

SOYA SAUCE:

There are 2 kinds. One is dark and the other is light. Both are used for seasoning foods. It cannot be made at home. It is easily available in bottles in shops.

VINEGAR:

It may be synthetic (acetic acid) or prepared from natural ingredients like rice, wine, sugar, fruits etc. The natural ones are better as the synthetically prepared chemical ones are too tart.

CHILLI SAUCE (RED OR GREEN):

This is a hot, spicy and tangy sauce made from red or green chillies, vinegar and seasonings. It is available ready made.

BLACK BEAN SAUCE:

This sauce is made from fermented black beans. It has a pungent and salty flavour. It cannot be made at home. It is available ready made in bottles at shops.

HOISIN SAUCE:

Also called peking or barbecue sauce. This is a thick brownish-red sauce. It is made form soybeans, spices, garlic and chilli peppers. It is used both in cooking and as a condiment. It is available ready made in bottles, at most shops.

WORCESTERSHIRE SAUCE:

It is a thin dark, piquant sauce used to season dishes. It is made from tamarind, dry fruits, garlic, ginger and spices.

OYSTER SAUCE:

Made from fresh oysters. Its special aroma and subtle sweetness enhance the flavours of most dishes. It is used not only in cooking but also as a condiment. Sprinkle a few drops over stir-fried iceberg lettuce & you will love it. Available in bottles & cans, it is best to refrigerate after opening.

SESAME OIL:

It is used as a flavouring, but not usually for cooking. It has a strong distinctive nutty taste & fragrant aroma. Only a small quantity is required. In cooked dishes a few drops of oil is usually added just prior to serving. It adds flavour to dips, salads and stir fry dishes.

STAR ANISE *(Chakri Phool)*:
The dried, hard, brown, star shaped fruit has a fennel flavour. It is an important ingredient used in five spice powder. It can be substituted with fennel seeds (saunf).

FIVE SPICE POWDER:
An aromatic blend of 5 Oriental spices 2 tsp peppercorns (saboot kali mirch), 3 star anise (phool chakri), 6 cloves (laung), 4" stick cinnamon (dalchini) and 3 tsp fennel (saunf). It is slightly sweet and pungent. Grind together to a powder, sieve & use.

CORNFLOUR:
It is a white powder, which is used to thicken sauces. Dissolve some cornflour in little tap water to make a paste and add it to boiling liquid. Remember to stir the sauce continuously, when the paste is being added. Also, stir the cornflour paste again before adding it to the dish.

AJINOMOTO (MONOSODIUM GLUTAMATE):
A white crystalline substance commonly known as MSG. It is used in Chinese cookery for enhancing the flavour of dishes.

DRY RED CHILLI:
Dry red chillies are easily available in markets. They are really hot. You can deseed them to decrease their heat.

CHINESE WINE:
There are many kinds of wine made from rice. Chinese wine can be substituted by ordinary dry sherry. Small amount of this wine adds a mild flavor.

BEAN CURD/TOFU:

It is prepared from soya bean milk. It resembles Indian Paneer in taste & looks. Thus, you can substitute paneer with tofu.

SNOW PEAS/MANGETOUT:

They belong to the pea family and are used in cooking just like we use French beans. Whole pod is edible. Snap off the stem end of pea pod and pull the thread.

SPRING ONIONS (HARA PYAZ):

These are also called scallions or green onions. In the absence of these, you can substitute them with regular onions. The green and white part, both are used. Add green part just at the end of cooking.

SESAME SEEDS (TIL):

These tiny, teardrop-shaped, flat seeds are quite tasteless in their raw state but impart a wonderful nutty flavour after roasting. These are cream and black in colour. The taste and visual appeal of food is enhanced, when coated with these seeds.

SEASONING CUBE & VEG STOCK:

Veg stock is an important agent for most soups and sauces. However, if you do not have stock ready or feel lazy to make a stock, you can use seasoning cubes mixed in water instead. Seasoning cubes are available as small packets. These are very salty, so taste the dish after adding the cube before you put more salt. Always crush the seasoning cube to a powder before using it.

SHALLOTS:

These are smaller onions, milder in flavour and belong to the onion family.

BAMBOO SHOOTS:
Fresh tender shoots of Bamboo plant are available rarely, but tinned bamboo shoots are easily available in good shops.

AGAR-AGAR:
This is a dried seaweed. The white fibrous strands require soaking and are used like gelatine. It is used for puddings and as a setting agent.

BEAN SPROUTS:
These are shoots of moong beans or soya beans. The texture is crisp.
To make bean sprouts at home, soak ½ cup of green beans (saboot moong dal) for about 8 hours. Discard water and tie in a muslin cloth. Keep them tied for 2-3 days, remembering to wet the cloth each day. When the shoots are long enough, wash carefully in water. Fresh bean sprouts will keep for 3-4 days if refrigerated in a plastic bag.

CHINESE CABBAGE *(wongnga bak/napa cabbage):*
It looks like a tightly packed cos lettuce. It has firm, pale green, crinkled leaves. If unavailable, ordinary cabbage can be used.

BOK CHOY (CHINESE CHARD):
A variety of Chinese cabbage. Also called spoon cabbage. It has dark green leaves with a white stalk and is used for stir frying. Both stalk and the leaves can be used. It is cooked only for a minute, so that it retains its colour and texture.

MUSHROOMS (Khumb):

There are many varieties which are used in Chinese cooking.

Fresh mushrooms are very tight, very firm and very white. You cannot see the gills underneath the cap. As the mushroom loses its moisture, the cap shrinks, exposing the gills. The most commonly available ones are called button mushrooms. Purchase fresh mushrooms no more than 1-2 days before using them, since they are highly perishable. Store in a loose plastic bag.

OYSTER MUSHROOMS:

These soft mushrooms are shaped like a fan. Delicous in flavour. Use them as soon as possible. Store in fridge.

DRIED MUSHROOMS:

May be white or black. To prepare dried mushrooms for cooking, soak them in hot water for atleast ½ hour to soften. They swell in size after soaking. Discard any hard stems. Cut into required size and use. They harbour a lot of dust and grit, so it is necessary to wash them well after soaking. They are added to dishes only for the last few minutes of cooking, to retain the crunchy texture. Used in soups and stir-fries.

About Noodles and Rice

Noodles are an important staple food in China. They are available in various kinds.

DRIED NOODLES: are made from plain flour (*maida*) or whole wheat flour (*atta*), with or without eggs. Straight as well as the coiled variety is available. They are usually cooked in boiling water with salt till almost done. Never fully done! Never overcook noodles as they turn thick and mushy on overcooking. They are cooked to an 'al-dente' stage (slightly *kaccha* with a little bite). Their cooking time is just 2 minutes for most of the varieties. Once they are strained, it is important to take the noodles out of cold water several times to arrest the cooking process, or they get overdone. A little oil should be sprinkled on the boiled noodles to prevent them from sticking.

FRESH NOODLES: are available with vegetable vendors. They are sold loosely like a tangled ball of wool. Since they are fresh and moist, the cooking time is much shorter than the dried noodles. These are usually cooked in boiling water for about a minute or even less sometimes.

RICE NOODLES/RICE VERMICELLI: These extremely thin noodles resemble long, translucent white hair. Rice noodles are just soaked in hot water for 5-6 minutes and then drained before use. When deep fried they explode dramatically into a tangle of airy, crunchy strands that are used for garnish. These are often called glass noodles. In the absence of these, the regular noodles or rice seviyaan can be used.

LONG/SHORT GRAIN RICE: Polished white rice that forms the basis of most Asian meals. The usual method of serving rice is simply boiled but sometimes, for variety and richness, boiled rice is fried with other flavouring ingredients, such as sliced green onions/scallions, chopped white mushrooms and garlic.

WHITE GLUTINOUS/STICKY RICE: This is a short-grain rice that sticks together when cooked because of high starch content. New rice can be used instead because the longer the rice is kept, the less sticky it gets. Glutinous rice is used in both savoury and sweet dishes and is usually soaked in water for about an hour before being cooked.

PARBOILED RICE (SELA RICE): Parboiled rice (Sela rice) is preferred to basmati rice for Chinese cooking. This is a hard grained, yellowish rice which does not stick at all after cooking.

RICE FLOUR: Ready-made rice flour is easily available in the market. To make it at home, grind raw rice *(kachcha chaawal)* to a smooth powder. Sift through a sieve *(channi)* to get a fine powder. *Adding small amounts of rice powder to a batter or coating mix, makes the food crisp. In its absence, it may be substituted with cornflour in batters.*

Chinese Cooking Utensils

YOU'LL BE GLAD YOU HAD IT!

Before actual cooking, check if you have all the necessary utensils. There are several items that are indispensable in Chinese cooking, e.g. wok and wok strainer etc. These essentials will help you create authentic flavours. Start with a few basic items.

COOKING UTENSILS

WOK:

It is a deep pan, round bottomed with a single or double handle on the sides. A wok is ideal not only for stir-frying but deep-frying and simmering also. Chinese cook everything in a wok - from soups to rice to main course dishes. Choose a heavy bottomed one. Non stick woks are also available.

The wok comes in various sizes, **the bigger the better.** **The most functional size is the 11-12 inch (28- 30 cm) round wok.** Sometimes it's fitted with a lid and an inner rack so you can steam vegetables and fish in it. The wok is deep, so you can boil rice and make soup in it. Its rounded sides provide enough red-hot surface for stir-frying foods quickly, usually in 3 to 5 minutes. The Indian kadhai is similar to a wok. You can use it in the absence of a wok. But I must tell you, buying a Chinese wok is much worth the investment!

WOK STRAINER:

A special strainer used to remove deep-fried pieces of food all together from oil at one time. Also useful for blanching food in hot water. Choose one which is slightly smaller than the wok. If not available, substitute with a single handle metal strainer.

STEAMING RACK (BAMBOO BASKETS):

An essential tool for steaming food, made of bamboo which allows steam rise efficiently. Place the steamer basket on a wok with ½" of boiling water as a single steamer or stack in several tiers so various dishes can be steamed at a time.

Colander *(steel ki big channi)* can be used instead of the steaming rack.

LADLE:

Perfect for stir-frying and braising any food in a wok. The preferred ladle has a sturdy joint and an easy-to-hold handle.

CHOPPING BOARD:

The Chinese use a big heavy chopping board on which they chop almost everything with a broad flat knife. An ordinary wooden board of a moderate size can be used.

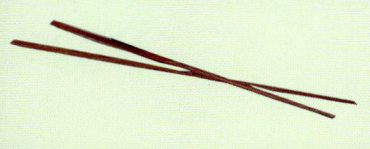

CHOPSTICKS:

These are thin long sticks, generally made of wood, and are used by the Chinese to eat with as well as to stir food while cooking.

Chinese Cooking Methods

STIR-FRYING:

Stir frying food, is to cook food on a high flame for a short period, **stirring continuously.** The ingredients are added to the wok in order of texture and cooking time. The hardest food is added at the start and the softer foods follow later, so stir frying of vegetables is done in sequence of their tenderness. E.g. onions are stir fried first, then french beans, then carrots, cabbage and so on. Each vegetable is stir fried for a few seconds, before adding the next vegetable. Stir-frying requires good temperature control and is easily learned through practice. The heat should be progressively raised for the addition of other ingredients. This is used for tender cuts of pork, poultry, seafood and vegetables. The ingredients are sliced, shredded, diced or minced, then stir fried in a wok using a spatula. Before you start stir-frying, remember to –

- Collect all ingredients required for the recipe.
- Slice all the veggies as required. Arrange in order of cooking.
- Marinade food if required, well in time.
- Measure liquids like oil, sauces and stocks.
- Blend any thickening agent (like cornflour) with stock or water and keep aside. Stir before adding to the wok.

PARBOILING:

To parboil means to partially cook food by boiling it briefly in water. Parboiling is used when cooking ingredients differ in tenderness and texture. The tougher varieties are added to boiling stock or water for a short time. They are then refreshed in iced water to set color and prevent overcooking. When the parboiled foods are cooked with more tender raw ingredients, the cooking time will then be the same. Whole carrots are peeled, beans are threaded and dropped in boiling water for ½ minute to parboil them. They are then cooled and cut into desired shapes. Cauliflower, broccoli and baby corns are some of the other vegetables which are generlly parboiled.

DEEP FRYING:

Ingredients are cut into even-sized pieces and dipped into a batter such as flour, beaten egg or bread crumbs. These are immersed in hot oil to cover, until cooked.

- A slice of ginger can be added to indicate the oil's temperature for deep frying. If the ginger turns golden, the oil is right for deep frying.
- Marinated ingredients should be drained before dipping into batter for frying.
- Add small quantities of ingredients to the oil at one time. This maintains the oil's temperature.
- Add some fresh oil to used oil before reusing. This prevents oil from discolouring.

How much oil to fill in the wok for frying?
Fill the wok or kadhai a little less than half with oil.

How hot should the oil be before frying.
Never fry in very hot smoking oil or cold oil. If the oil gets too hot, remove from fire and wait for 2 minutes. If the food is added to very hot oil it can turn into a dark mess. If the oil is not hot enough, then food absorb a lot of oil!

STEAMING:

Steam is made from boiling water and the heat of the steam cooks the food.

The food is placed on a rack kept above boiling water from which the steam comes. The food does not touch the water. Dim sum are usually steamed. We require Chinese steaming baskets for steaming. These are made from bamboo and consist of two baskets and a lid. They come in various sizes. A new bamboo steamer should be soaked in water overnight before it is used the first time. Chinese metal steamers are also available and can be used.

HOW TO STEAM?

Bamboo steamers are placed into a wok containing an inch or so of vigorously boiling water. Fill 1" level of water in a wok or a pot and bring it to a boil. Place the ingredients in the wooden steamer, stack them and cover tightly with a lid. Steam the food over appropriate heat: meats over high heat, egg dishes and puddings over low heat. Then remove the lid carefully before serving. This is how we steam dim sum, steamed fish, dumplings.

IF STEAMER BASKETS ARE UNAVAILABLE, THEN HOW DO WE STEAM?

Cook food by placing in a colander (metal strainer with big holes/*steel ki badi channi*). Place the colander over boiling water in a slightly smaller pan. Cover the colander while steaming. Steaming helps retain flavour, shape, colour, texture and nutritional value.

Vegetable Cutting Methods

CHOPPING: TO CUT INTO SMALL PIECES
The vegetable is cut into small pieces. Holding on to the vegetable firmly, cut the vegetable lengthwise into slices and then holding on firmly, give the sliced vegetable a quick turn at a right angle. Now cut the sliced vegetable again into slices which will result in finely chopped pieces. Onions and tomatoes are usually chopped in the recipes.

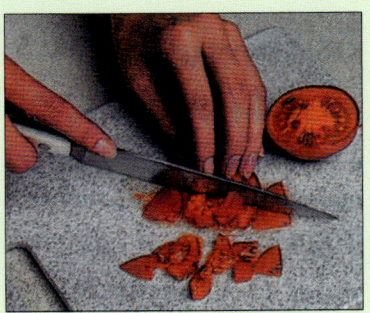

SHREDDING: TO CUT INTO THIN, LONG PIECES
The vegetables are cut into thin, strips or shreds. Spinach, lettuce, cabbage are all shredded. Carrot can be grated on the big holes of a grater to get shredded carrot.

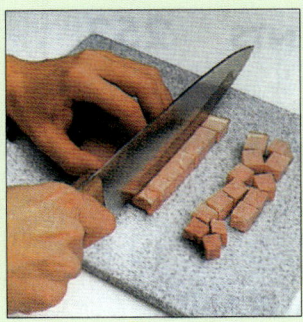

DICING: TO CUT INTO VERY SMALL SQUARES
The vegetables are cut into dice or small cubes. The vegetables are first cut lengthwise into ¼ or ½ inch thick strips/fingers and several such strips/fingers are kept together and further cut into ¼ inch pieces.

DIAGONAL SLICES: TO CUT VEGETABLE SLICES IN A SLANTING MANNER

The vegetables are cut into thin slices in a slanting manner in such a way that there are more exposed surfaces. Vegetables such as asparagus, carrots, celery or French beans are usually diagonally sliced.

JULLIENE: TO CUT INTO THIN MATCH STICK LIKE PIECES

The vegetables are cut into thin slices lengthwise. The slices are stacked together and cut lengthwise to get thin match sticks. Carrots and cucumber juliennes look good.

SLICING: TO CUT COMPLETELY THROUGH THE VEGETABLE TO GET SLICES

The vegetables are cut into thin slices. The thickness depends on what is specified in each individual recipe. Tomatoes, carrots, mushrooms, onions etc. are sliced in quite a few recipes.

RINGS AND HALF RINGS: TO CUT THE VEGETABLES WIDTHWISE INTO ROUNDS

Vegetables like onions or capsicums are cut widthwise to get rounds. The onion slices are then separated to give full rings. For half rings, cut the vegetables first into half and then cut widthwise to get half rings. When opened the half rings look like thin strips of onion and can be used as shredded onion also.

CARROT OR RADISH FLOWERS: These flowers are usually seen in Chinese dishes. If the dish requires round slices of carrots, cut the carrot into round flowers instead. It enhances the look of stir fried dishes.

For carrot flowers, peel a thick, big carrot. Cut into two pieces to get 2 shorter lengths. Firmly holding the carrot upright, with a small sharp knife, make 1/8 inch broad and deep lengthwise cuts along the length of the carrot. Tilt the knife slightly to take out the thin long piece from the cut to get a groove. Make 2-3 more grooves leaving equal space between them. Carefully, cut the carrot into round slices.

CARROT LEAVES:
CUT A CARROT INTO VERY SLANTING SLICES.
Cut a big carrot into very thin and very slanting slices. Make "V" notches on the side to get leaves.

 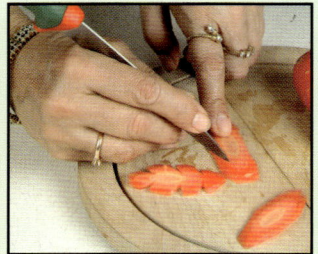

TRIANGULAR PIECES: cut a capsicum into 4 pieces lengthwise. Cut each piece at an angle, to get a small triangle of about 1". Cut the left over strip into half, giving a slant cut in the opposite direction at the centre to get 2 more triangles. Smlarly you could get triangular pieces of tomatoes also. Coloured capsicums really look good when cut into this shape.

Simple Vegetable Garnishes

Always make vegetable carvings and garnishes before you begin a recipe.

VEGETABLE SHREDS: It looks beautiful on soups, salads and fried rice.
Cut the green portion of spring onion into very fine shreds. Shred as thinly as posssible. Put the fine shreds ino chilled water for a few minutes. Iced water will make the onion curl tightly.

ONION WATERLILIES: It can be used to garnish stir - fries.
Use bulbous green onions or small white onions. Peel, wash & cut off green tops. Cut adjoining V-shapes around the onion, making sure the knife cuts through to the center. Separate the 2 halves by gently pulling apart; put into a bowl of iced water for several hours or overnight in the refrigerator to allow the onions to open out. Onions will keep for several days in water in the refrigerator. The onions may be left white or tinted with a few drops of food coloring added to the water. To achieve the two-toned effect, soak onions in lightly colored water; then dip into a very strong soloution of the same color. Trim off the root.

CUCUMBER SPRINGS: It can be used to garnish salads or any platter.

Use small tender cucumbers that have very few seeds. Cut the cucumber into approximately 3-inch pieces, discarding the ends. Poke a wooden chopstick right through the cetner of cucumber. Holding a small sharp knife at a slight angle, make the first cut all the way through to the center of the cucumber until the knife hits the chopstick. Continue cutting around the cucumber turning the chopstick as the cucumber is being cut until the end is reached.Remove the chopstick and pull the end of the cucumber gently so it forms a "spring". The ends may be joined to form a circle or the spring can be placed around a dish as a border. A slice of red radish placed between every second coil adds extra color.

Clear your doubts...
How to Use Chopsticks

Come in various lenghts and styles. China, Korea and Vietnam also use chopsticks and each country has different types of chopsticks. Traditional Japanese chopsticks are made of bamboo or cedar. These materials were used so that the fine surface of the pottery would not be scratched and also Japanese like the touch of wood rather than metal. Chopsticks are all-purpose handy utensils for oriental cooks. Use them to reach the bottom of deep pots, pans and bowls and to stir, beat, whisk, turn food and lifte all sorts of food.

To Use?

1. Chopsticks are placed on the chopstick rest thinner ends on your left. Hold the center with your right fingers.
2. Pick up and add left fingers beneath. Immediately slide your right fingers towards right ends.
3. Now hold steadily, the upper stick between thumb and forefinger, the lower stick between the tip of third finger and the base of thumb, with middle finger lifting the upper stick.
4. Release left fingers. Fix the lower stick and move the upper stick up and down using the fore finger and middle finger.

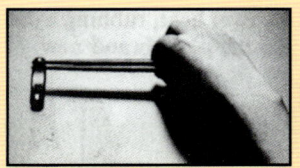   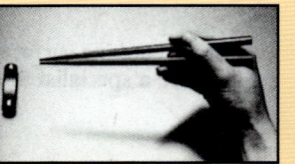

WHAT IS THE DIFFERENCE BETWEEN LIGHT SOYA SAUCE AND DARK SOYA SAUCE?

Both are rich in flavour, but the lighter variety is generally used when you do not want to disturb the colour of the dish.

SEASONING THE WOK/KADHAI...

It is important to do it, to avoid rice or noodles from sticking to the kadhai. Heat about ½ cup oil in a wok/kadhai to a smoking point. Remove from fire. Holding the wok carefully swirl the hot oil around to grease all the sides. Remove oil from the wok. Add ¼ tsp of salt. With a cut potato or onion, rub this salt all around the wok.

THE QUANTITY OF SOYA SAUCE DEPENDS UPON ONES OWN LIKING OR TASTE.

The amount of soya sauce can be increased or reduced according to the desired colour of the dish. Remember, soya sauce is salty, so keep a check on the salt when you increase the quantity of soya sauce.

HAS YOUR SOYA SAUCE BOTTLE BEEN LYING AROUND UNUSED FOR A COUPLE OF MONTHS OR MORE?

Soya sauce gets concentrated and thick on keeping for too long. Adding even a little bit makes the dish turn blackish. So add it gradually and see it for yourself, how much the dish needs. Check for colour and salt as you keep adding more.

AJINOMOTO MAY BE INJURIOUS TO HEALTH!

Avoid ajinomoto, the Chinese salt, as far as possible. Use it only if neccessary. Usually just a pinch is enough. When you double the quantity of the dish, do not double the quantity of ajinomoto.

ALWAYS USE A BIG PAN OR WOK TO STIR-FRY. WHY?

This avoids mashing or breaking the food into bits.

JUST A POINT:

A Chinese dish will have all the vegetables and meat cut in the same shape, e.g. to prepare any dish with noodles, all the vegetables are always cut into thin long strips. For fried rice, everything is diced — cut into small squares.

REMOVING SEEDS FROM CAPSICUMS:

Cut into half lengthwise and again into half lengthwise. Cut the white portion and discard. Proceed as required.

HOW TO PARBOIL VEGETABLES:

Sometimes vegetables are slightly cooked in salted water and then added to the dish. Whole carrots are peeled, beans are threaded, cauliflower or broccoli is broken into florets and dropped in boiling water for one minute to parboil them. They are then cooled and cut into desired shapes.

THIN SAUCE - HOW TO USE CORNFLOUR TO THICKEN IT?

Sometimes, the sauce may appear a little thin. To thicken it, dissolve a little extra cornflour in some tap water and add it to the boiling sauce. Remember to stir the sauce continuously, when the cornflour paste is being added. Bring to a boil and stir on medium flame for 1-2 minutes.

THE RIGHT WAY TO CUT CABBAGE:
Cut into half first and then again into half. Keeping the cut side, flat on a board, chop or cut into thin long pieces.

HOW TO PEEL GARLIC QUICKLY ?
Hit garlic clove with the flat side of a heavy knife to crack the skin, which will then slip off easily. Finely chop garlic with a knife.

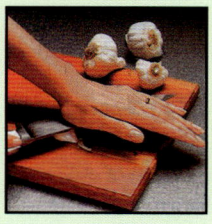

WHEN WE SAY FLORETS OF CAULIFLOWER. WHAT DOES IT MEAN?
Remove the extra stalk, leaving about ½" stalk near the base of the head. Cut the flower into two halves, right through the stalk. Break into pieces into florets as the recipe demands.

Soups

Seasoning Cubes... What are they?

These are small packets of a special powder which is full of flavour. It can be mixed in water and used as stock for any recipe which requires stock or 1 cube can be added to 2-4 cups of soup for great flavour. These are very salty, so taste the dish after adding the cube before you put more salt. Always crush the seasoning cube to a powder before using it. It blends better.

Garnish for Soups

FRIED NOODLES
½ cup raw noodles can be deep fried on medium heat till golden. Top a cup or a bowl of soup with 1-2 tbsp of these fried noodles. Store these fried noodles in an air-tight container and use whenever required.

SPRING ONION GREENS
Chop a green stalk of spring onion very finely and top soup with 1 tsp of these.

GOLDEN TOFU CUBES
Cut tofu or paneer into tiny cubes of ¼" and deep fry till golden.

Helpful Hints for Soups

If the soup appears thin, dissolve 1-2 tsp cornflour in a little tap water and add to the boiling soup. Stir on low medium heat till it thickens.

Vegetables in soup taste good if they are crunchy & crisp-tender. Never boil the soup too much after adding the vegetables as the vegetables turn soft on doing so.

A seasoning/stock cube added to the soup makes a lot of difference in the taste. Keep stock cubes in the fridge.

Fresh Vegetable Stock

Makes 6 cups

1 onion - chopped, 1 carrot - chopped, 1 potato - chopped

4-5 french beans - chopped or ½ cup chopped cabbage

½ tsp crushed garlic - optional, 1 tsp crushed ginger, ½ tsp salt, 7 cups water

1 Mix all ingredients and pressure cook for 10-15 minutes.
2 Do not mash the vegetables if a clear soup is to be prepared. Strain and use as required.

Quick Vegetable Stock

Soup cubes or seasoning cubes may be boiled with water and used instead of the stock, if you are short of time. These seasoning cubes are easily available in the market and are equally good in taste.

Makes 2½ cups

1 vegetable seasoning cube (maggi, knorr or any other, SEE NOTE), 2½ cups of water

1 Crush 1 seasoning cube roughly in a pan. Add 2½ cups of water and give one boil. Use as required.

Note: The seasoning cube has a lot of salt, so reduce salt if you substitute this stock with the fresh stock. Check taste before adding salt.

Sweet Corn Vegetable Soup

Serves 6

1 cream style sweet corn tin (460 gm), about 2½ cups

1 spring onion (hara pyaz) - finely chopped along with the greens

¼ cup carrot - finely chopped, ¼ cup cabbage - finely chopped

1 tbsp vinegar, 2 tbsp green chilli sauce, 1 tbsp red chill sauce

2 tsp level salt, ¼ tsp pepper, a pinch of ajinomoto

4 tbsp cornflour dissolved in ¾ cup water

1. Dissolve cream style corn in 9 cups water in a deep pan. Bring to a boil. Boil for 5-7 minutes.
2. Add vinegar, green and red chilli sauce. Simmer for 1-2 minutes.
3. Add salt, pepper and ajinomoto to the soup. Add cornflour paste and cook for 2-3 minutes till the soup thickens.
4. Add the vegetables- onions, carrot and cabbage to the simmering soup. Simmer for 1 minute. Serve hot.

Sweet Corn Soup with Fresh Corn

For fresh corns, grate 5 large corns and pressure cook grated corn with 9 cups water and 1½ tbsp sugar to give 2 whistles. Keep on low heat for 6-7 minutes. Remove from heat and let it cool down. Proceed from step 2.

Hot & Sour Soup

It is made hot with black pepper and red chillies.

Serves 4-5

CHILLI-GARLIC PASTE

3 dry red chillies - deseeded and soaked in water for 10 minutes
2 flakes garlic, 1 tsp vinegar, 1 tbsp oil, 2 tbsp water

OTHER INGREDIENTS

2 tbsp oil, 1-2 tender french beans - sliced very finely (3-4 tbsp)
1-2 tbsp dried mushrooms or 2-3 fresh mushrooms - chopped
½ cup chopped cabbage, ½ cup thickly grated carrot
6 cups water
2 vegetable seasoning cubes (maggi) - powdered, see page 29
1 tsp sugar, 1 tsp salt, ½ tsp pepper powder, or to taste
1½- 2 tbsp soya sauce, 1½ tbsp vinegar
5-6 level tbsp cornflour mixed with ½ cup water

1. For the chilli-garlic paste, soak dry, red chillies in a little water for 10 minutes.
2. Drain the red chillies. Grind red chillies, garlic, vinegar and oil roughly with 2 tbsp water in a small coffee or spice grinder.
3. If dried mushrooms are available, soak them in water for ½ hour to soften. Wash thoroughly to clean the dirt in them. Cut away any hard portion and then cut into smaller pieces.
4. Heat 2 tbsp oil. Add beans and mushrooms. Stir fry for 1-2 minutes on high flame. Add cabbage and carrots. Stir for a few seconds.
5. Add the water and the seasoning cubes. Add chilli-garlic paste, sugar, salt, pepper, soya sauce and vinegar. Boil for 2 minutes.
6. Add cornflour paste, stirring continuously. Cook for 2-3 minutes till the soup turns thick. Serve hot.

How much Soya Sauce to add?

Soya sauce becomes darker in colour and concentrated on keeping. If you have an old bottle of soya sauce lying around, use sparingly and watch the colour of the soup. More can be added later according to the desired colour.

Wonton Soup

The wontons can be deep fried and served as appetizers before dinner. When added to soups, they are not fried but cooked (poached) in the boiling stock.

Serves 6

WONTON WRAPPERS

1 cup plain flour (maida), ½ tsp salt, 1 tbsp oil, a little water (chilled)

WONTON FILLING

½ of a small onion - finely chopped, ½ carrot - chopped very finely

8 french beans - chopped very finely or 1 cup chopped mushrooms

½ cup cabbage - finely chopped, a pinch of ajinomoto (optional)

½ tsp white pepper, salt to taste, ½ tsp sugar, 1 tsp soya sauce

WONTON SOUP

6 cups stock, (see pg 30) 2 spring onions - chopped finely alongwith the greens

1 tbsp soya sauce, 1 tsp white pepper, 1 tsp sugar, ¼ tsp ajinomoto (optional)

1. To prepare the wonton wrappers, sift plain flour and salt.
2. Add oil and rub with finger tips till the flour resembles bread crumbs. Add chilled water gradually and make a stiff dough. Knead the dough well for about 4-5 minutes till smooth. Cover dough with a damp cloth. Keep aside for ½ hour.

3. To prepare the filling, heat 1 tbsp oil. Stir fry onions, for a few seconds.
4. Add all other vegetables. Stir fry for 1-2 minutes. Add ajinomoto, pepper, salt, sugar and soya sauce. Mix. Remove from fire. Cool filling before making wontons.
5. Divide the dough into 4 balls. Roll out each ball into thin chappatis. Cut ½" from all the sides to get a square piece.
6. Cut the big square piece into 2" small squares. (a) Place some filling in centre. (b) Fold in half by lifting one corner & joining to the opposite corner to make a triangle. Press sides together. (c) Fold a little again, pressing firmly at both sides of the filling, but leaving corners open.
7. Bring 2 corners together, and cross over infront of the filling. Brush lightly with water where they meet, to make them stick. Keep wontons aside. (The wontons may be folded into different shapes like money bags, nurses caps or envelopes).
8. To serve soup, boil vegetable stock, add the prepared wontons. Cover and cook for 12-15 minutes on low flame till they float on top.
9. Add spring onions, soya sauce, pepper, sugar and ajinomoto. Simmer for 1-2 minutes. Remove from fire. Serve hot.

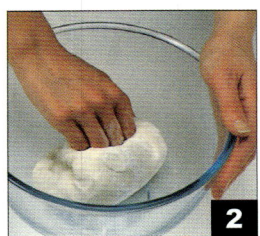
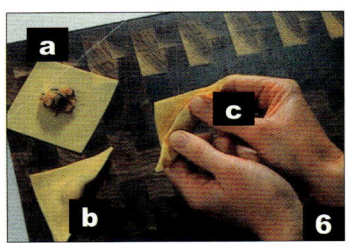

Talomein Soup

Serves 4

4 cups vegetable stock (see page 30)
½ carrot - peeled, 3-4 cabbage leaves - roughly torn
¼ cup dried noodles or ½ cup fresh noodles
1 tsp salt, or to taste, ½ tsp each of sugar, black pepper
1 tsp soya sauce, a pinch ajinomoto (optional)
2 tbsp cornflour dissolved in ½ cup water

1. Boil 5 cups of water in a large pan. Add 2 tsp salt and 1 tsp sugar to the water. Add peeled carrot to the boiling water. Boil. Keep on boiling for 1-2 minutes. Drain. Refresh in cold water. Cut into diagonal slices. Keep aside.
2. Mix stock, noodles, salt, pepper, sugar, soya sauce, ajinomoto in a pan. Give 1-2 boils.
3. Mix cornflour with ½ cup water in a bowl. Add this cornflour paste, stirring continuously to the pan boiling with stock.
4. Add carrots and cabbage. Bring to a boil. Remove from fire. Serve.

Mushroom Crispy Rice Soup

Serves 6

½ cup boiled rice, 1 cup sliced fresh mushrooms (6-7)

1 onion - sliced, 1 tsp ginger paste, 1 tsp white pepper, 1¼ tsp salt or to taste

6 cups water, 2 veg seasoning cube, see page 29

2 tbsp soya sauce, 1 tbsp vinegar, 2 tsp sugar

4 tbsp cornflour dissolved in ¼ cup water, 2 tbsp oil

1. Boil rice and spread on a tray. Deep fry rice till golden brown.
2. Slice mushrooms finely.
3. Heat oil. Add sliced onion and stir till light brown and slightly crisp on the edges. Add sliced mushrooms. Stir fry for 2 minutes.
4. Add ginger paste. Stir fry for ½ minute.
5. Add water and crushed seasoning cube.
6. Add all other ingredients except cornflour paste. Boil.
7. Add cornflour paste. Cook for 1 minute till the soup turns thick. Serve soup garnished with deep fried rice.

Note: Add 1 tbsp cornflour mixed with 1 tbsp water in the end if slightly thicker soup is desired.

Starters

Tips for Handling Starters

◆ JUST A TIP! ◆

HOW DO YOU STEAM A STARTER WITHOUT A STEAMER BASKET?

To steam, fill a deep pan with a little water, say upto 1" level. Keep it on fire to boil the water. Put a steel strainer (colander) on the pan of water. Put the food as it is or in another utensil like a thali, on the strainer and cover the strainer with a lid. Lower the heat to medium. Do not steam on very low heat as the water will not boil and no steam will form.

WHAT IS THE RIGHT WAY TO FRY A STARTER OR ANYTHING IN GENERAL?

Heat oil in a kadhai, but if it starts to smoke, shut off heat. Let it cool down a bit and return to heat. Dry your food well before frying. Fry in batches as too much food in the oil lowers the temperature of the oil and the food absorbs a lot of oil if the oil is not hot enough.

HOW MUCH OIL SHOULD I PUT IN THE KADHAI FOR FRYING A STARTER OR ANYTHING IN GENERAL?

Fill the kadhai a little less than half with oil. If there is too much oil, it bubbles and flows over. If it is too little, the food is not fried properly.

Kimchi Salad

The popular Chinese salad. It is always served at the start of a Chinese meal in most Chinese restaurants.

Serves 4

½ of a medium cabbage (300 gms), 1 tbsp ginger match sticks

SYRUP

¼ cup sugar, ¼ cup water, 1 tsp salt, ¼ tsp red chilli flakes

¼ tsp pepper, 1 tsp crushed garlic, 2 tbsp vinegar

ADD LATER

½ tsp coarse salt (sendha namak), ¼ tsp white pepper

1 tsp soya sauce, 1-2 tbsp tomato ketchup, 1-2 tsp red chilli sauce

1. Cut cabbage into 1" square pieces. Put in a big bowl. Add ginger match sticks also.
2. Boil ¼ cup of water with ¼ cup sugar. Simmer for 2 minutes. Add salt, red chilli flakes, pepper, garlic and vinegar. Remove from fire immediately and pour the hot syrup on the cabbage in the bowl. Cover with a lid, pressing the cabbage with the lid. Keep aside for 2 hours.
3. Strain the cabbage. Leave it in the strainer for 15 minutes for the syrup to drain out completely.
4. Add all the other remaining ingredients to the cabbage and toss lightly so that the sauces coat the cabbage. Serve at room temperature.

Spring Rolls

Serves 4

SPRING ROLL WRAPPERS

1 cup plain flour *(maida)*, ½ cup cornflour, ½ tsp salt, 2 tbsp oil, a little water (chilled)

VEGETABLE FILLING

1 onion - chopped finely, 8 french beans - shred diagonally

½ cup moong bean sprouts, ½ carrot - grated

½ cup shredded cabbage, ½ cup chopped capsicum

a pinch of ajinomoto (optional), ½ tsp white pepper

salt to taste, ½ tsp sugar, 1 tsp soya sauce, 2 tbsp oil

♦ **BEAN SPROUTS** ♦

To make bean sprouts soak ½ cup of green beans (saboot moong dal) for about 8 hours. Discard water and tie in a muslin cloth. Keep them tied for 2-3 days, remembering to wet the cloth each day. When the shoots are long enough, wash carefully in water.

1. To prepare the wrappers, sift plain flour, cornflour and salt.
2. Add oil and water gradually, mixing to make a dough. Knead very well till smooth and elastic. Keep dough aside for ½ hour.
3. Makes very small balls from the dough. Roll into thin rotis (rounds) 3"-4" in diameter.
4. Heat a tawa & put 1 thinly rolled roti on it. Cook on both sides for 2-3 seconds. Keep rotis covered in a moist cloth or aluminium foil in a box.

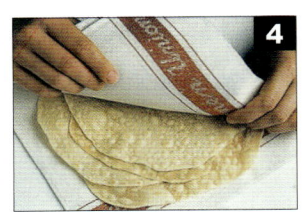

TiP

* Put wrapped rolls, joint ends down & the weight of the rolls will help them stick well.

* Always keep the spring roll wrappers covered with a moist, clean cloth or aluminium foil or cling wrap until needed, to prevent them from drying out.

It is better to shred cabbage and other vegetables as finely as possible for the filling.

5. For filling, heat oil. Add onion, cook till soft. Add beans, cook for a minute.
6. Add sprouts and stir fry for 1 minute. Add carrot, cabbage, capsicum, ajinomoto, pepper, salt and sugar. Stir fry for 1 minute. Add soya sauce. Mix. Check seasonings.
7. To assemble wrapper, spread a roti on a flat surface. Cut 1" from all the sides to get a square piece.
8. Spread some filling thinly on the upper portion. Fold in ½" from the right and left sides.
9. Holding on, fold the top part to cover the filling. Roll on to get a rectangular parcel; making sure that all the filling is enclosed.
10. Seal edges with cornflour paste, made by dissolving 1 tsp of cornflour in 1 tsp of water. Chill for ½ hour in the fridge, it gives better shape.
11. Repeat for the remaining rotis and filling. Cover all with a plastic wrap/cling film to prevent drying out. Keep aside till serving time.
12. Heat some oil in a large frying pan for deep frying. Reduce heat and put the rolls, folded side down first in oil. Turn sides, to make it crisp and golden from all sides. Drain on paper napkins/absorbent paper. Cut into 2 pieces with a sharp knife and serve hot with chilli sauce.

Shredded Potatoes

A popular snack. Saucy and crisp golden potato fingers. Remember to refry the fingers before putting them in the sauce at the time of serving.

Serves 4

2 large potatoes

3 spring onions - white part finely chopped and greens cut diagonally into 2" pieces

4-5 green chillies - slit lengthwise and deseeded

4-5 flakes garlic - crushed, optional

1 tsp soya sauce, 1 tbsp red chilli sauce

3 tbsp tomato ketchup, ¾ tbsp vinegar

2 tsp honey, ½ tsp each of salt and white pepper

BATTER

¼ cup flour (maida), ¼ cup cornflour

½ tsp salt, ¼ tsp pepper

a pinch of ajinomoto

½ tsp soya sauce, a pinch or drop of orange red colour

How to deseed green chilli?

Cut the green chilli into half lengthwise Scrape away the seeds from both pieces and then chop or use as required.

Chop white portion of spring onions and cut green into diagonal pieces !

Chop the white bulb finely and cut the green portion in a slanting manner. Use both separetely.

1. Wash potatoes and cut into ½" thick slices. Cut each slice into ¼" wide fingers. Soak them in 4-5 cups cold water with 2 tsp salt and juice of 1 lemon, for 15 minutes. Strain and wipe dry on a clean kitchen towel. Sprinkle ¼ tsp white pepper and 3-4 tbsp cornflour on them to absorb excess water.
2. For batter- mix flour, cornflour, salt, pepper, ajinomoto, soya sauce and colour. Add just enough water, about 5-6 tbsp, to make a batter of a thick pouring consistency, such that it coats the potatoes. Keep batter aside for 10 minutes.

3. Dip fingers of potatoes in the batter and deep fry in 2 batches to a golden orange colour. Check that they get properly cooked on frying. Keep the fried fingers spread out on a plate till the time of serving. Do not pile them on each other - they turn limp!
4. Heat 1 tbsp oil in a pan. Add white of spring onion. Stir till light brown. Remove from fire. Add the green chillies and garlic. Stir till garlic starts to change colour.
5. Add soya sauce, chilli sauce, tomato ketchup and vinegar.
6. Return to fire. Add honey, salt, pepper and 3 tbsp water. Mix well. Remove from fire. Keep aside.
7. At serving time, heat oil for refrying the potatoes. Add the fried potatoes in hot oil and refry in 2 batches for a minute. Remove from oil and put in the pan of sauces. Add spring onion greens. Mix very well for a minute on high heat. Check salt. Serve hot.

Steamed Momos

Serves 12

DOUGH

¾ cup plain flour (maida), ¼ cup rice flour or cornflour, 1 tbsp oil, ½ tsp salt

FILLING

1 onion - finely chopped, 6 mushrooms - chopped very finely
1 tsp ginger-garlic paste, 2 green chillies - finely chopped
1 large carrot - very finely chopped or grated
2½ cups very finely chopped cabbage (1 small cabbage)
1 tsp salt & ½ tsp pepper powder, or to taste, 1 tbsp vinegar, ½ tsp soya sauce

RED HOT CHUTNEY

2-3 dry whole, Kashmiri red chillies - desseded and soaked in ¼ cup warm water for 10 minutes, 6-8 flakes garlic, 1 tsp saboot dhania (coriander seeds)
1 tsp jeera (cumin seeds), 1 tbsp oil
½ tsp salt, 1 tsp sugar, 3 tbsp vinegar, ½ tsp soya sauce

> **U should Know...**
> The preferred way to steam momos or any vegetable is to steam it on medium high heat. Do not keep the heat low otherwise the water does not boil properly and enough steam is not formed, leaving them undercooked. For even cooking make sure that the DUMPLINGS are not touching the water when you place them in the steamer.

1. Sift maida with salt. Add oil and knead with enough water to make a stiff dough of rolling consistency, as that for puris. Keep in a cool place covered with a damp cloth for 30 minutes.

2. Heat 2 tbsp oil in the kadhai for the filling. Add the chopped onion. Fry till it turns soft. Add mushrooms and cook further for 2 minutes. Add green chillies, carrot & ginger-garlic paste. Mix well and add the cabbage. Stir fry on high flame for 3 minutes. Add salt, pepper, vinegar and soya to taste. Remove from fire and keep the filling aside to cool.
3. Take out the dough and form marble sized small balls. Roll out flat, as thin as possible into small rounds of 2½" diameter.
4. Put 1 heaped tsp of the filling on one side and fold over to form a semicircle. Stick the edges with water. Pleat the joint edges and then slightly fold the pointed ends to give it a little rounded shape. Make all momos. Keep aside.
5. To steam, place the momos in a greased steamer or in an idli stand or in a greased colander (steel channi with big holes) and steam for 10 minutes. See page 18.
6. Remove momos to a plate.
7. For chutney, grind the soaked red chillies along with the water, garlic, dhania, jeera, oil, salt and sugar to a paste. Add soya sauce and vinegar to taste.

IF STEAMER BASKETS ARE UNAVAILABLE, THEN HOW DO WE STEAM?
Cook food by placing in a colander (flat strainer with big holes/ steel ki badi channi). Place the colander over boiling water in a slightly smaller pan. Cover the colander while steaming. Steaming helps retain flavour, shape, colour, texture and nutritional value.

Lotus Wings

Serves 4

200 gm lotus stem (bhein) - peeled & cut diagonally into thin slices

2 spring onions - cut white part into rings and greens into 1" diagonal pieces, (keep greens separate)

1-2 green chillies - chopped finely, 4-5 flakes garlic - crushed (optional)

¼ tsp each of ajinomoto, salt, pepper, sugar, 1 tbsp soya sauce

1 tbsp red chilli sauce, 1½ tbsp tomato ketchup, ½ tbsp vinegar

1 tbsp honey, 1 tbsp coriander - chopped

BATTER

4 tbsp plain flour (maida), 4 tbsp cornflour

2 flakes garlic - crushed to a paste, ½ tsp salt, ¼ tsp pepper

1. Cut lotus stem diagonally into thin slices.
2. To parboil lotus stem, boil 4 cups water with 1 tsp lemon juice and 1 tsp salt. Add sliced lotus stem to boiling water. Boil for 2 minutes. Strain. Refresh in cold water. Strain and keep aside. Wipe dry on a clean kitchen towel.

3. Cut white bulb of spring onion into rings and cut green part diagonally into 1" pieces.
4. For batter- mix maida, cornflcur, garlic, salt & pepper. Add just enough water, to make a batter of a thick coating consistency, such that it coats the slices.
5. Dip each piece in batter. Deep fry in two batches to a golden yellow colour. Keep aside.
6. Heat 2 tbsp oil in pan. Reduce heat. Fry the green chillies and garlic till garlic just starts to change colour. Add white of spring onions. Add ajinomoto, salt, pepper and sugar.
7. Remove from fire. Add soya sauce, red chilli sauce, tomato ketchup and vinegar. Return to fire. Stir for a few seconds.
8. Add greens of spring onion. Stir for a few seconds.
9. Add honey and mix.
10. Add fried lotus stem and coriander. Mix well till dry and the sauce coats the lotus stem. Remove from heat. Serve hot.

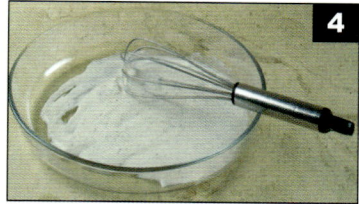

TiP

You can fry the lotus stem 3-4 days or even more in advance. When you take them out of oil after frying, spread them out on a tray in a single layer. Do not heap them. Let them turn cold. Store in a zip lock bag or box in the freezer compartment of the fridge.

Accompaniments to Starters & Soups...

Sizchuan Sauce

Makes ¼ cup

¼ of a onion - very finely chopped
1 tsp celery - very finely chopped
PASTE (GRIND TOGETHER)
3 dry red chillies - broken into small pieces
2- 3 flakes of garlic, 4 tbsp tomato ketchup, 1 tbsp oil
½ tsp soya sauce, ¼ tsp salt, 1½ tbsp vinegar

1. Mix the paste, onion, celery and ¼ cup water in a pan. Cook, stirring constantly till it boils. Simmer for 2 minutes. Serve at room temp.

Hot & Sour Sauce

Make ¾ cup

¾ cup water, 2 tbsp vinegar, 1 tsp pepper powder
salt to taste, 1 tbsp cornflour, ½ tsp sugar, or to taste

1. Mix all the ingredients in a pan. Cook, stirring constantly till it boils. Simmer for 2 minutes on low heat. Remove from fire.

Green Chillies in Vinegar

Makes ¼ cup

¼ cup white vinegar, ½ tsp salt, ½ tsp sugar
2-3 drops soya sauce, 2-3 green chillies

1. Chop green chillies finely.
2. Mix all the other ingredients except green chillies. Heat on fire till it is just about to boil.
3. Add green chillies. Stir to mix well.
4. Remove from fire. Serve in a small bowl.

Sweet & Sour Sauce

Makes 1½ cups

½ cup tomato ketchup, ¼ cup vinegar
2 tbsp sugar, 1 cup water, 2 tbsp cornflour
½ tsp white pepper, ½ tsp salt, or to taste

1. Mix all the ingredients in a pan. Cook, stirring constantly till it boils. Simmer for 2 minutes on low heat. Remove from heat.

Red Sesame Dip

2 tbsp oil, 2 tsp sesame seeds (til)

2-3 flakes garlic - chopped very finely

2 dry red chillies - broken into small pieces & deseeded

4 tbsp ready made tomato puree

ADD LATER

¼ tsp salt, ½ tsp sugar, 1½ tbsp vinegar

½ tsp soya sauce, 1 tsp sesame oil (optional)

1. Heat oil. Add sesame seeds. Stir till golden.
2. Reduce heat, add garlic & red chillies. Stir till red chillies turn blackish & garlic changes colour.
3. Add tomato puree. Cook for 3-4 minutes or till dry and oil separates. Remove from fire. Let it cool. Put chilli-tomato mixture in a mixer.
4. Add salt, sugar, vinegar, soya sauce and 2 tbsp water to the mixer. Grind all together to a paste. Check salt.
5. Remove to a bowl. Add sesame oil. Mix. Serve.

Sweet Chilli Dip

A thin dipping sauce which goes well with Chinese starters.

2½ tbsp sugar, ¼ cup water

1 tbsp honey, 1 tsp soya sauce

4 tbsp white vinegar, 1-2 tbsp oil

6-8 flakes garlic - crushed to a paste (1 tsp)

½ tsp red chilli powder

¼ tsp salt

1-2 fresh or dry red chillies - very finely chopped with a knife

1. Boil sugar and water till sugar dissolves. Stir continuously.
2. Add honey.
3. Add all other ingredients and remove from fire. Serve at room temperature.

Chinese Saucy Dishes

Potato Strings in Ginger Sauce

Serves 4

2 potatoes - sliced very thinly to get juliennes
3 capsicums - sliced very thinly to get juliennes
3½ tsp ginger paste, 2 onions - chopped finely, 1 tsp salt, ¾ tsp pepper
1 tsp soya sauce, 2 tsp tomato ketchup, 2¼ tbsp cornflour mixed with ½ cup water
2 vegetable seasoning cubes (maggi, knorr or any other, see page 29)

Juliennes
It means to cut into thin match stick like pieces

1. To make stock with cubes, crush 2 vegetable seasoning cubes and mix with 2 cups of water in a saucepan. Give one boil and keep aside.
2. Peel potatoes. Wsah and cut each into thin slices, and cut each slice further into very thin fingers to get juliennes. Wipe dry on a kitchen towel. Put in a bowl and sprinkle 2-3 tbsp cornflour to absorb the excess moisture. Mix well. Cut capsicum also to get thin fingers.
3. Heat oil in a wok. Deep fry some shredded potatoes at a time. Fry in batches till golden brown and crisp. Drain on paper napkins. Keep them spread out. Repeat to fry the remaining potato strings.
4. Heat 4 tbsp oil in a kadhai. Add ginger paste. Cook on low flame for 1-2 minutes.
5. Add the chopped onion, cook till golden. Add salt and pepper. Stir fry for a few seconds. Add soya sauce, ketchup. Add the prepared seasoning water or stock. Give one boil.
6. Add cornflour paste, stir till the sauce just starts to get thick. Remove from fire and keep aside till serving time. At serving time, bring the sauce to a boil. Simmer for 1-2 minutes. Add fried potatoes and capsicum. Mix well and serve hot immediately.

Vegetable Manchurian

Vegetable balls in a thin brownish sauce.

Serves 4

MANCHURIAN BALLS

1 cup grated cauliflower (gobhi), ¼ cup diced or grated carrots (gajar)

¼ cup finely grated cabbage (bandgobhi)

1-2 slices bread - grind in a mixer to get fresh bread crumbs

1 tbsp cornflour, 1 tbsp flour (maida)

¼ tsp ajinomoto - optional, salt and pepper to taste, 2-3 tbsp milk

MANCHURIAN SAUCE

2 tbsp oil, 1" piece ginger - crushed to a paste

5-6 flakes garlic - crushed (or 1 tbsp ginger-garlic paste)

2 green chillies - chopped, ½ onion - very finely chopped

1 tbsp soya sauce, 1½ tbsp tomato ketchup, 2 tsp vinegar

½ tsp salt, ¼ tsp pepper, 2 tbsp cornflour - dissolved in ½ cup water

1 spring onion greens - chopped finely, to garnish

What are fresh crumbs?
To make fresh bread crumbs, tear bread into small pieces. Churn in a mixer grinder to get fresh crumbs.

1. Mix all ingredients of the balls, adding only ½ of the fresh bread crumbs mixture first. (Remaining bread crumbs may be added if balls fall apart on frying.) Add enough milk so that the balls bind together easily. Make oval balls. Flatten each ball slightly.
2. Deep fry 3-4 pieces at a time on medium flame. Reduce flame after the balls turn light brown and fry till cooked and brown. Keep aside.
3. To prepare the manchurian sauce, heat 2 tbsp oil in a wok or kadhai. Add ginger and garlic. Fry on low flame for 1 minute.
4. Add green chillies and onions. Cook till they turn light brown.
5. Reduce heat and add soya sauce, tomato ketchup, vinegar, salt and pepper. Stir for 1 minute.
6. Add 1½ cups of water. Boil. Keep on slow fire for 2-3 minutes.
7. Dissolve cornflour in ½ cup water and add to the above sauce, stirring continuously. Cook till slightly thick. Keep the sauce aside.
8. To serve, boil the sauce. Add the balls to the manchurian sauce and keep on slow fire for one minute till the balls are heated through. Serve hot sprinkled with finely chopped spring onion greens with fried rice or noodles.

Caution!

Fry only 3-4 balls at a time in hot oil on medium heat. Too many balls at a time in oil, reduces the temperature of oil. End result...balls break on frying.

Tofu in Hot Garlic Sauce

Serves 3-4

200 gm tofu (paneer can be used instead)

BATTER

3 tbsp cornflour, 3 tbsp plain flour (maida)

1 tsp soya sauce, ½ tsp garlic or ginger paste

¼ tsp each of pepper & salt

¼ tsp ajinomoto, optional, ¼ cup water

GARLIC SAUCE

20 flakes garlic - chopped & crushed roughly in a small spice grinder (1½ tbsp)

2 dry, red chillies - broken into two, deseeded and chopped with a knife or scissors

½ onion- chopped, 1 capsicum - cut into tiny cubes

4½ tbsp tomato ketchup, 2 tsp red chilli sauce, 2 tsp soya sauce

½ tsp pepper, 1 tsp salt, a pinch sugar, 2 tsp vinegar

¼ tsp ajinomoto (optional), 1½ cups water

2 tbsp cornflour mixed with ½ cup water

> **TiP**
>
> *Never add garlic to very hot oil, it will turn brown and lose most of its flavour.*

1. To prepare the sauce, peel and grind the garlic to a very rough paste in a small grinder. Keep the mixer on just for 1-2 seconds. Do not make a smooth paste.
2. Heat 3 tbsp oil. Remove from fire. Add garlic and red chilli bits. Stir till garlic starts to change its colour.
3. Add onion, cook till soft.
4. Add tomato ketchup, red chilli sauce, Soya sauce, pepper and salt. Cook for 1 minute on low heat. Add sugar, vinegar and ajinomoto.
5. Add capsicum.
6. Add water, give one boil.
7. Add cornflour paste, stirring all the time. Cook for 2 minutes on low heat. Check salt. Remove from heat. Keep sauce aside.
8. Cut tofu or paneer into 1" cubes.
9. Make a thick coating batter by mixing all ingredients of the batter with a little water.
10. Dip tofu or paneer pieces and deep fry to a golden colour. Keep aside.
11. At serving time, add fried tofu to sauce & boil for 2 minutes. Serve with rice.

Problems to Avoid !

Do not drop tofu in the centre of wok as it will cause the hot oil to splatter. Gently slide in from the sides of the wok.

TiP

If using paneer instead of tofu, you can forget frying the paneer if you wish!

Veggies in Szechwan Sauce

Serves 4

100 gms tofu or paneer - cut into ¼" thick triangular pieces - sprinkled with ¼ tsp salt & white pepper and
1 tbsp cornflour, 4-5 florets of broccoli or cauliflower, 4-6 babycorns - cut into 2 pieces diagonally
1 carrot - sliced very diagonally and then cut into 2 pieces, 6-8 leaves of bokchoy or spinach
1 tbsp of dried black mushrooms or 3-4 fresh mushrooms - cut into 2 pieces
1 capsicum - cut into 1" pieces, 2 tbsp bamboo shoots (tinned) - cut into thin diagonal slices

SZECHWAN SAUCE

4 tbsp oil, 1 onion- cut into 1" pieces, 1 tsp red chilli sauce, 2 tsp soya sauce
2 laung (cloves) - crushed, 3 tbsp ready-made tomato puree, 2 tbsp tomato ketchup
¼ tsp pepper, ½ tsp salt or to taste, 1 tsp sugar, or to taste, ¼ tsp ajinomoto (optional)
1½ cups water mixed with 2 seasoning stock cubes (maggie or knorr), see page 29
3 tbsp cornflour mixed with ½ cup water

PASTE

1 tbsp chopped garlic, 1 tsp vinegar
2 dry, red chillies - break into bits & remove seeds and soak in water for 10 minutes

1. If using dried mushrooms, put them in a pan. Cover with water. Boil. Simmer for 2 minutes. Remove from fire. Keep aside for 10 minutes. Wash several times. Break off any hard stem portion & discard. Wash several times scrubbing well, to clean the hidden dirt.
2. If using bokchoy or spinach, trim the stem, remove any discoloured leaves. Tear into 2" pieces.
3. Boil 4-5 cups water with 1 tsp salt. Remove from fire. Add broccoli or cauliflower, baby corns, carrots and bokchoy or spinach. Leave veggies in hot water for 1-2 minutes and strain. Refresh in cold water and keep aside till serving time.
4. Grind all ingredients written under paste in a small grinder.
5. Heat 4 tbsp oil in a pan. Shallow fry the tofu till golden. Remove tofu from pan.
6. To prepare the sauce, heat 2 tbsp oil again in the same pan. Remove from fire. Add garlic-red chilli paste. Stir till garlic starts to change its colour.
7. Add onion. Saute for 1 minute. Shut off the flame add laung, tomato puree, ketchup, red chilli sauce, Soya sauce, pepper, salt, sugar and ajinomoto.
8. Return to fire and cook for 1 minute on low heat.
9. Add water mixed with seasoning cubes, give one boil.
10. Add cornflour paste, stirring all the time. Cook for 2 minutes on low heat. Add bamboo shoots. Remove from heat. Keep aside till serving time.
11. To serve, heat the sauce. Add the soaked mushrooms, tofu, blanched vegetables and capsicum. Bring to a boil and simmer for 1 minute. Serve.

American Chopsuey with Vegetables

Serve this dish quickly as the crispy fried noodles soak up the sauce on keeping for too long hence turning the dish limp.

Serves 4

- 100 gm crispy noodles (see on the right side)
- 1 carrot - parboiled
- 8 french beans - parboiled, 1 green chilli - shredded
- 1 capsicum - shredded, 1 onion - shredded
- ¾ cup cabbage - shredded
- ½ cup bean sprouts, 2 cups water
- ½ tsp white pepper
- salt to taste
- 5 tbsp oil, ¼ tsp ajinomoto (optional)
- 1 tsp soya sauce
- 1 tsp vinegar
- 4 tbsp tomato ketchup
- 3 tbsp cornflour dissolved in ½ cup water

Crispy Noodles

Serves 4

<u>100 gms noodles - boiled</u>
<u>1 tbsp flour, 2 cups oil for frying</u>

Boil noodles as given on page 87. Sprinkle flour on noodles to discard any water present. Heat about 2 cups of oil. Add half of the noodles. Stir, turning sides till noodles are golden in colour and form a nest like appearance. Remove from oil. Drain on absorbent paper. Fry the left over noodles in the same way. Cool and use or store in an air tight tin till further use.

1. Prepare crispy noodles as given on page 67.
2. Scrape carrot, string french beans or snow peas.
3. Boil 3 cups water with 1 tsp salt. Parboil vegetables by dropping the whole carrot and french beans in boiling water. Strain after half a minute. Wash with cold water. Let them cool down.
4. Shred all vegetables into thin long strips - capsicum, onion, cabbage, carrot and french beans.
5. Heat 5 tbsp of oil. Except sprouts add all the remaining vegetables. Stir fry for 2 minutes.
6. Add sprouts, pepper, salt and ajinomoto. Stir fry for 1 minute.
7. Add soya sauce, vinegar and tomato ketchup. Cook for ½ minute.
8. Add 2 cups water. Bring to a boil.
9. Add cornflour paste, stirring continuously. Cook for about 2 minutes, till thick. Keep aside.
10. To serve, spread crispy noodles on a serving platter, keeping aside a few for the top.
11. Top with the prepared vegetables.
12. Sprinkle some left over crispy noodles on it. Serve hot.

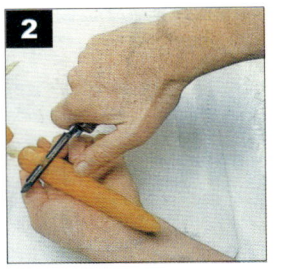

Cauliflower in Pepper Sauce

Serves 2-3

½ of a small cauliflower - cut into ¾" florets (1½ cups)

2 tbsp oil, a pinch of salt, ½ tsp pepper, pinch of ajinomoto (optional)

greens of 1 spring onion - cut into ½" pieces

SAUCE

1 white portion of spring onion - chopped

¼ tsp ginger paste, ¼ tsp chopped garlic

6 peppercorns (saboot kali mirch), 1 tsp freshly ground black pepper

½-1 tsp soya sauce, 1 tsp vinegar, ¼- ½ tsp salt or to taste

a pinch of ajinomoto, 2 tbsp oil

MIX TOGETHER

1½ cups water, 1 vegetable seasoning cube (maggi or knorr)

PASTE

1¾ tbsp cornflour, ¼ cup water

100% sure cauliflower is free of insects!

When not too sure especially during summers or rainy season, just boil half a pan of water with 2 tsp salt. Add cauliflower pieces to boiling water. Remove from fire. Let it sit in salted water for 10 minutes. Remove from the water with a flat spoon with holes (chhara). Never strain! You might carry the insects back with the vegetable. Put the cauliflower in  *tap water to stop heat from making it mushy. Pat dry on a clean kitchen towel and use.*

1. Cut cauliflower into ¾" florets with a little stalk.
2. Chop white portion of spring onion. Cut the green portion into ½" pieces.
3. Crush 1 vegetable seasoning cube and add to 1½ cups of water in a saucepan. Give one boil and keep aside.
4. Mix cornflour with water to a smooth paste. Keep aside.
5. Heat 2 tbsp oil in a wok or a kadhai and add cauliflower.
6. Stir fry the cauliflower for 3-4 minutes on medium heat till brown specs appear on the cauliflower.
7. Add a pinch of salt, ¼ pepper and pinch of ajinomoto. Keep aside.
8. Heat 2 tbsp oil. Reduce heat and add white portion of spring onion, ginger paste, chopped garlic and peppercorns. Cook till garlic changes colour. Reduce heat, add black pepper, soya sauce, vinegar, salt and ajinomoto.
9. Add water mixed with a seasoning cube. Give one boil.
10. Add the prepared cornflour paste. Cook till sauce thickens slightly. Keep aside till serving time.
11. Add fried cauliflower and greens of spring onion. Remove from fire. Serve hot.

TiP

Pat dry the washed cauliflower nicely on a kitchen towel to avoid a mushy texture.

This dish can also be made with broccoli instead of cauliflower.

When we say florets of cauliflower, what does it mean?

Remove the extra stalk, leaving about ½" stalk near the base of the head. Cut the flower into two halves, right through the stalk. Break into pieces into florets as the recipe demands.

Chinese Stir Fries

HOW TO STIR-FRY FOOD:

Stir frying food, is to cook food on a high flame for a short period, **stirring continuously.** Stir frying of vegetables is done in sequence of their tenderness. e.g. onions are stir fried first, then french beans, then carrots, cabbage and so on. Each vegetable is stir fried for a few seconds, before adding the next vegetable.

Stir-frying is one of the most popular methods of Chinese cooking. A wok is best for stir-frying but a large frying pan can be used. As stir-frying is so quick it's important that you have all your ingredients prepared before you start cooking.

For successful stir-frying, heat your wok until very hot, then add the oil. Swirl the wok to coat the surface and continue to heat until the oil is almost smoking before adding the food. Following this procedure will ensure that the food does not stick to the wok. An exception to this is when the first ingredients to be added to the wok are garlic, spring onions, ginger or chillies. Add these ingredients immediately after adding the oil or they will burn when added to very hot oil.

Spicy Honey Veggies

A delightful and colorful semi-dry dish with a crunchy texture!

Serves 4

¾ tsp salt and ¼ tsp pepper, or to taste

a pinch ajinomoto (optional)

2-3 tsp red chilli sauce, 2½ tbsp tomato ketchup

1 tsp soya sauce, 1½ tbsp vinegar

3 tbsp cornflour dissolved in ½ cup water with 1 seasoning cube, see page 29

1 large carrot, 8-10 mushrooms - trim stalks and keep whole

8-9 baby corns - keep whole if small and divide into two lengthwise, if thick

1½ cups cauliflower or broccoli - cut into small, flat florets (¼ of a small flower)

1 onion - cut into 8 pieces and separated

1 capsicum - cut into ½" cubes

4 tbsp oil, 2-3 dry, red chillies - broken into bits & deseeded

15 flakes garlic - crushed

3-4 tsp honey, according to taste

1. Boil 4 cups water with 1 tsp salt. Peel carrot. Drop the whole carrot, mushroom, cauliflower and baby corns in boiling water. As soon as the boil returns, remove from fire and strain the vegetables. Refresh veggies in cold water.
2. Cut parboiled (half cooked) carrot into ¼" thick round slices or flowers. To make flowers, make slits or grooves along the length of the boiled carrot, leaving a little space between the slits. Cut the grooved carrot widthwise into slices to get flowers. Cut capsicum into ½" pieces. Cut onion into fours and separate the slices.
3. Dissolve cornflour in ½ cup water. Add seasoning cube and keep aside.
4. Heat oil in a kadhai. Reduce heat. Add broken red chillies and garlic.
5. Stir and add onion, mushroom, baby corns, carrots and cauliflower. Add salt and pepper. Add ajinomoto. Stir for 1-2 minutes on high flame. Add capsicum. Reduce heat.
6. Stir & add chilli sauce, tomato ketchup, soya sauce, honey & vinegar. Lower heat & stir for ½ minute.
7. Add the dissolved cornflour and seasoning cube. Cook till the vegetables are crisp-tender and the sauce coats the veggies. Serve immediately.

TiP

How much soya sauce to add?

Soya sauce adds colour too, besides enhancing flavour. Different types of soya sauce are available - dark & light. Also, if the soya sauce has been lying around in the house for a few months, it gets concentrated and even a small quantity of it, imparts a dark colour to the food. It is always better to add a lesser quantity of the sauce and add more later according to the colour of the dish. Too much soya sauce spoils the colour of the dish sometimes!

Babycorn Aniseed

Babycorns fragrantly flavoured with fennel, can be served as a side dish or a snack.

Serves 4

200 gm babycorns

BATTER

3 tbsp cornflour, 2 tbsp plain flour (maida)

2 tbsp suji (semolina), 1 tbsp saunf (aniseeds or fennel) - powdered

½ tsp soya sauce, ½ tsp garlic or ginger paste

½ tsp salt, ¼ tsp ajinomoto, optional, ¼ cup water, approx.

RED CHILLI - GARLIC PASTE

3-4 flakes garlic, 2 dry red chillies - broken into bits and deseeded

1 tsp saunf (fennel)

OTHER INGREDIENTS

2 spring onions - chop white and cut greens separately into ¼" pieces diagonally

¾ tsp salt, ¼ tsp ajinomoto, 1 tbsp soya sauce, 2 tbsp tomato sauce, ½ tbsp vinegar

2 tsp cornflour mixed with ½ cup water

1. Cut a thin slice from the flat end (not the pointed end) from each baby corn. Wash and wipe well on a clean kitchen towel.
2. Make a thick coating batter by mixing all ingredients of batter with a little water.
3. For the red chilli - garlic paste, soak all ingredients together in ¼ cup water for 10 minutes and grind to a paste along with the water.
4. Heat 4 tbsp oil in a pan. Remove pan from fire and swirl or rotate the pan so as to coat the bottom of the pan nicely with oil. Return to fire.
5. Dip babycorns in the prepared batter and shallow fry half of the babycorns in a pan on medium flame, turning sides, till golden and cooked. Remove on paper napkins and keep aside. You can also deep fry the vegetable.
6. Heat the remaining oil in the pan. Add white of spring onions. Cook for a minute.
7. Add the prepared red chilli - garlic paste. Stir for a minute.
8. Add ¼ cup water. Stir.
9. Reduce heat. Add salt, ajinomoto, soya sauce, tomato sauce and vinegar.
10. Add cornflour paste. Stir for a minute till thick. Add greens of onions and babycorns. Mix well and serve hot.

Is the oil ready for deep frying?

Put a tiny piece of bread in hot oil. If the oil sizzles and the bread turns golden within 30 seconds and comes to the surface, go ahead and fry baby corn. Extra hot oil will turn the bread dark brown. If the oil is not hot enough, the bread will quietly remain at the bottom and it will absorb too much oil during browning.

Hoisin Stir Fry Okra

A dry dish. Crispy fried okra (bhindi) tossed in a tempting hoisin sauce. Hoisin sauce is available at all leading food stores. In the absence of it you can use tomato ketchup.

Serves 4

250 gms okra (bhindi) - slice into 2 pieces lengthwise

1 onion - cut into 8 pieces

1 tsp ginger-garlic paste (½" piece ginger and 4 flakes of garlic - crushed)

2-3 tbsp hoisin sauce

1 tbsp soya sauce, 2 tbsp red chilli sauce, ¼ tsp salt

1 tsp cornflour mixed with ¼ cup water, oil for frying

THIN COATING BATTER

½ cup cornflour, 2 tbsp plain flour (maida)

1 tsp ginger-garlic paste, ½ tsp salt, ¼ tsp white pepper powder

1 tsp soya sauce, ½ tsp vinegar, 1 tsp lemon juice

¼ cup water, approx.

Is it tender!

Break the pointed tip of an okra. If the tip snaps off easily, the okra is tender and fresh.

1. Wash and wipe dry bhindi with a clean napkin. Cut into 2 long pieces lengthwise.
2. Mix all ingredients of the batter in a big bowl, adding enough cold water (about ¼ to ½ cup) to get a coating batter of pouring consistency. Do not make the batter too thick or too thin.
3. Dip the bhindi in batter and mix well. The batter should coat the vegetable lightly. If not, sprinkle 2 tbsp more cornflour on the vegetable and mix well.
4. Deep fry in hot oil putting one piece at a time to get crisper bhindis. Do not pick up a handful of pieces to fry together. Add only that much quantity of bhindi which the kadhai can hold (fry in batches). Deep fry till pale golden on medium heat. Remove on paper napkin.
5. Heat 1 tbsp oil in a pan and stir fry onions for 2 minutes.
6. Add the ginger-garlic paste and saute for half a minute.
7. Shut off the flame, add the hoisin sauce, soya sauce, red chilli sauce and ¼ tsp salt. Mix well.
8. At serving time, return to fire and add the cornflour paste. Add fried bhindi. Mix gently for a minute. Serve immediately.

TiP

Stir frying takes only fe *minutes Deep fry okra an* *keep aside till serving time. S* *fry the fried okra with sauce* *at the time of serving.*
Hoisin sauce also makes a *excellent base for dips. Mix* *with seasonings and try it.*

Stir fried Snow Peas/Beans

Use any combination of vegetables that you have on hand or just cottage cheese (paneer) and spring onions to make this quick stir-fry. Adjust the vegetables you use, accordingly season to suit your taste.

Serves 4

200 gms snow peas or french beans

50-75 gm paneer - cut into thin, 2" long pieces

1 onion, 4 tbsp oil

1½" piece ginger - cut into jullienes or thin match sticks (1½ tbsp)

3-4 green chillies - shredded (cut into thin pieces lengthwise)

OTHER INGREDIENTS

1½ tbsp soya sauce, 2½ tbsp tomato ketchup

1 tbsp vinegar, 1 tsp red chilli sauce

2 tbsp sherry or wine (optional)

1½ tbsp worcester sauce, ½ tsp salt, ¼ tsp pepper, or to taste

½ tsp ajinomoto (optional)

1 tbsp dry bread crumbs, optional

SNOW PEAS/MANGETOUT:

They belong to the pea family and are used in cooking just like we use French beans. Whole pod is edible. Snap off the stem end of pea pod and pull the thread.

TO CUT PANEER INTO THIN 2" LONG PIECES

1. Remove strings/threads from snow peas or beans.
2. If using snow peas, keep whole. If using french beans, cut each into 1½-2" pieces. If using beans, boil 4-5 cups water with 1 tsp salt and 1 tsp sugar. Add beans and boil for 1-2 minutes. Strain.
3. Peel onion. Cut into half and then cut widthwise to get half rings, which when opened become thin long strips and you get shredded onion.
4. Heat 4 tbsp oil in pan. Add onion, cook till golden.
5. Add ginger jullienes and green chillies. Stir fry for 1-2 minutes till ginger turns golden.
6. Add snow peas or beans and stir fry for 3-4 minutes till vegetable turns crisp-tender. Keep the vegetable spread out in the pan while stir frying.
7. Reduce heat. Add soya sauce, tomato ketchup, vinegar, red chilli sauce, sherry, worcester sauce, salt, pepper and ajinomoto.
8. Add paneer and mix well.
9. Add bread crumbs. Stir fry on low heat for 2 minutes till the vegetable blends well with the sauces. Serve hot.

Noodles & Rice

HOW TO BOIL NOODLES CORRECTLY TO AVOID THEM FROM TURNING MUSHY?

Never overcook noodles as they turn thick & mushy. They should be a little hard when you drain them. Some noodles like glass noodles made from rice or fresh noodles available at the vegetable vendors do not need boiling. They are added to boiling water and the fire is shut off immediately. After being left in hot water for 2-3 minutes, they are strained when slightly soft. Noodles are always rinsed in cold water, they have to be taken out of cold water several times till the water is no longer hot. If not done this way, they get slightly overcooked if they remain warm. It is always better to sprinkle some oil on them to prevent them from sticking to each other.

SHOULD YOU SOAK RICE BEFORE COOKING?

The traditional way is to soak rice for 20-30 minutes before cooking. But I have experienced that soaking makes the rice extra soft and so there are great chances for the grains to break when the rice is sauteed in oil when making a pullao. The best way is to wash the rice and let it be in the strainer for 20-30 minutes. The rice stays moist in the strainer and remains full grained on cooking.

Perfect Boiled Noodles

Serves 2-3

100 gm noodles, 6 cups water, 1 tsp salt, 2 tsp oil

1. In a large pan, boil 6-8 cups water with 2 tsp salt and 1 tbsp oil. Add noodles to boiling water.
2. Cook uncovered, on high flame for about 2-3 minutes only. Stir once in between.
3. Remove from fire before they get **overcooked**. Drain.
4. Put in cold water. Strain. Apply 1 tbsp oil on the noodles and spread in a tray till further use.

Chinese Steamed Rice

Serves 2-3

1 cup uncooked long grained rice, 2 cups water, 1 tsp salt, 1 tbsp refined oil

1. Clean and wash rice thoroughly.
2. Heat water with salt and oil. When it boils, add the rice.
3. Slow down the fire, keep a griddle (tava) under the pan of rice and cook for about 15 minutes on very low heat, until the water is absorbed and the rice is cooked.

Perfect Boiled Rice

Serves 2

1½ cups uncooked rice, 2 tsp salt, 6-8 cups water

1. To boil rice, clean and wash 1½ cups rice. Soak rice for 10 minutes.
2. Boil 6-8 cups of water with 2 tsp salt. Add rice.
3. Cook, uncovered, over a medium flame, stirring occasionally, until the rice is just tender but not **overcooked**.
4. Drain the rice and let it stand in the strainer for 5 minutes. Fluff with a fork.
5. Spread on a tray and keep aside for atleast 1 hour before you stir fry them.

Note: **a.** About 4 cups of cooked rice is ready. The rice should be boiled **2-3 hours** before making fried rice. Hot rice when stir fried tends to get mushy.

b. Parboiled (sela), good quality rice should be used. Long grained rice is better. 1 cup uncooked rice will give about 2½ cups cooked rice.

Chilli Garlic Noodles

Stir fried noodles, which will be an excellent accompaniment to any wet dish.

Serves 3-4

200 gm dried noodles or 400 gms fresh noodles, 3 tbsp oil, 1 tsp crushed garlic
3 dry, whole red chillies - broken into bits, ½ tsp red chilli flakes
a pinch of sugar ½ tsp salt or to taste, 2 tsp soya sauce, ½ tsp white pepper

1. To boil noodles, see page 87.
2. Cut the dry red chillies into small bits or pieces.
3. Heat 3 tbsp oil. Add garlic. Stir.
4. Remove from fire, add broken red chillies and red chilli flakes.
5. Return to fire and mix in the boiled noodles. Add salt, pepper, sugar and a little soya sauce. Do not add too much soya sauce.
6. Mix well with the help of 2 forks. Fry for 2-3 minutes, till the noodles turn a pale brown. Serve hot.

TiP

By drizzling soy sauce from the sides of the wok, a savory aroma will be released and enhance the flavor.

Haka Noodles with Vegetables

Serves 4

CHILLI NOODLES

400 gms fresh noodles - boiled in salted water for just 2 minutes & spread in a tray

4 tbsp oil, 4-5 dry, whole red chillies - broken into bits

½ tsp chilli flakes or powder, 2 tsp salt, ½-1 tsp soya sauce

VEGETABLES

1 capsicum - shredded finely

1 carrot - cut into fine juliennes or match sticks, 1 cup shredded cabbage

6-8 flakes garlic - crushed and chopped - optional

2 spring onions or 1 small onion - shredded

2 tbsp bean sprouts - optional

1-2 tbsp dried black mushrooms soaked & washed thouroughly or finely sliced fresh mushrooms

1 tsp salt & ½ tsp pepper, ½ tsp ajinomoto - optional, 1 tbsp vinegar

1. Break red chillies into bits/pieces.
2. Heat 4-5 tbsp oil. Remove from fire, add broken red chillies and red chilli flakes or powder.
3. Return to fire and mix in the boiled noodles. Add salt and a little soya sauce. Do not add too much soya sauce. Fry for 2-3 minutes, till the noodles turn a pale brown. Keep the fried noodles aside.
4. To prepare the vegetables, shred all vegetables.
5. Heat 2 tbsp oil. Reduce heat and add garlic. Cook for ½ minute.
6. Add vegetables in sequence of their tenderness - onions, sprouts, mushrooms, carrot and cabbage stir fry for 2 minutes. Add vinegar. Add capsicum.
7. Add ajinomoto, salt and pepper. Cook for ½ minute. Slide in the noodles and mix well. Serve.

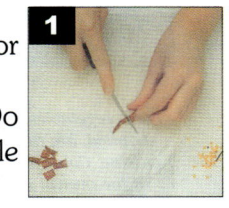

TiP

Bean sprouts keep best when stored in the fridge.

Glutinous Rice

A sticky rice dish! It's a little sweet because of the honey added to it.

Serves 6

1½ cups uncooked sticky rice (new short grained rice may be used)

2 tbsp oil, 1 onion - sliced, 2 flakes garlic - crushed

2 spring onions - chop white and green part separately

2 green chillies - chopped, ½ cup peas (matar)

½ tsp jeera powder (cumin powder), ½ tsp dhania powder (ground coriander)

1 tsp saunf - crushed, 1 tsp salt, ½ tsp pepper

MIX TOGETHER

3 cups veg stock or 3 cups of water mixed with 1 vegetable seasoning cube, see page 29

3 tbsp honey, 3 tbsp soya sauce

TiP

Other varieties of rice, such as white Basmati rice or long grain rice can be used in this dish but you will need to adjust the cooking time accordingly.

1. Wash and soak rice. Keep aside.
2. Mix all the ingredients written under mix together in a bowl. Keep aside.
3. Heat oil in a large deep pan, add sliced onion & garlic and stir-fry for 4-5 minutes or until onion is soft.
4. Add white part of spring onion, green chillies and peas.
5. Add jeera powder, dhania powder, crushed saunf, salt and pepper. Stir-fry for 1 minute.
6. Drain rice and add to the pan. Stir for 3-4 minutes on low heat.
7. Add stock-honey mixture and green of spring onion. Stir and bring to a boil.
8. Reduce heat and cook covered for 10 minutes or until rice is done and the water gets absorbed. Serve hot.

Vegetable Chow Mein

Serves 4

200 gm dry noodles or 400 gms fresh noodles - boiled, see page 87

2-3 flakes garlic - crushed (optional)

1 onion - sliced, 1 carrot - shredded

1 cup shredded cabbage, 1 capsicum - shredded

1 tsp salt, 1 tsp white pepper

a pinch of sugar

¼ tsp ajinomoto (optional)

2-3 tsp soya sauce, 1 tbsp vinegar

1½ tsp chilli sauce

TiP

You can use fresh or dried noodles for this recipe. Both taste equally good.

1. In a large pan, boil 8-10 cups water with 2 tsp salt and 1 tbsp oil.
2. Add noodles to boiling water. Cook uncovered, on high flame for about 2 minutes only. Remove from fire before they get **overcooked**. Drain.

3. Wash with cold water several times. Strain. Apply 1 tbsp oil on the noodles and spread them on a greased tray.
4. Shred all vegetables into thin long strips. To shred onions, peel and cut into half. Cut each half into thin semi circles to get thin long strips of onion. To shred carrots, grate on the thick side of the grater.
5. Heat 4 tbsp oil. Add sliced onion. Stir fry for 1- 2 minutes. Add garlic. Mix.
6. Stir fry carrots for ½ minute. Add cabbage and capsicum. Mix.
7. Add salt, pepper, sugar and ajinomoto. Mix.
8. Add boiled noodles. Sprinkle soya sauce and mix well with 2 forks so that all the ingredients are mixed well. Add more soya sauce for a darker colour. Check salt.
9. Add vinegar and chilli sauce. Stir fry for 1 minute. Serve.

Vegetable Fried Rice

Serves 4

1½ cups uncooked rice - boiled, see page 88

2 flakes garlic - crushed (optional), 2 green chillies - chopped finely

2 green onions - chopped till the greens, keep greens separate

¼ cup very finely sliced french beans

1 carrot - finely diced (cut into tiny cubes)

½ big capsicum - diced (cut into tiny cubes)

1 tsp salt, ½ tsp pepper, ¼ tsp ajinomoto (optional)

1-2 tsp soya sauce (according to the colour desired) 1 tsp vinegar (optional)

1. To boil rice, see page 88.
2. Heat 2 tbsp oil. Add garlic, green chillies and white of onions. Stir.
3. Add beans, stir for a minute. Add carrots. Stir fry for 1 minute. Add capsicum. Stir to mix. Add salt, pepper and ajinomoto. Mix well. Add rice. Reduce heat. Sprinkle soya sauce and vinegar on the rice.
4. Mix well using 2 forks. Add greens of onions. Stir fry rice for 2 minutes. Serve.

TiP

My Secret

It is recommended to cook fried rice in a small portion at a time to avoid the rice turning into a hash. If you want to double the serving, make the recipe twice for best results.

Sela rice (parboiled rice) is preferred to basmati rice for Chinese cooking. This is a hard grained, yellowish rice which does not stick at all after cooking.

Desserts

Toffee Apples

Serves 4

3 delicious golden or red apples

oil for deep frying

CARAMEL COATING

1 cup sugar, 2 tbsp oil

2 tsp sesame (til) seeds

½ cup water

BATTER

½ cup plain flour (maida)

2 tbsp rice flour or cornflour

½ tsp baking powder

1. Put the sugar, 2 tbsp oil and ½ cup of water in a pan and cook stirring on low flame till sugar dissolves. Increase to a high flame.
2. When the mixture begins to bubble, stir continuously to prevent the sugar from burning.
3. Continue stirring the pan until the syrup is light brown in colour. Take a little syrup in a spoon and check carefully - it is going to be very hot! If it feels sticky when felt between the thumb and the fore finger and forms a thread when the finger is pulled apart, it is ready.
4. Remove from the heat, add the sesame seeds and mix well. Keep the caramel syrup aside.
5. Sift the plain flour, rice flour or cornflour and baking powder in a bowl. Add about ½ cup water to get a smooth, thick batter of a coating consistency.
6. Peel and cut the apples into four pieces. Remove the seeds. Cut each piece further into 2 pieces if the apples are big.
7. Heat oil for frying. Coat the apple pieces evenly with the batter and deep fry 5-6 pieces together at one time, in hot oil until golden.
8. Keep a serving bowl filled with ice-cubes ready and cover with water.
9. Put the fried apples in the caramel syrup and coat evenly. Drain well and dip immediately into the ice-cubes bowl. Keep for a few minutes till the caramel coating hardens.
10. Drain thoroughly. Keep aside till serving time.
11. Serve plain or with ice cream.

Note: While this dish takes a little time to prepare and cook, it is well worth the effort. Other fruits, such as bananas and pears, are also delicious cooked in this way.

Glossary of Names/Terms

HINDI OR ENGLISH NAMES USED IN INDIA	AS ENGLISH NAMES AS USED IN USA/UK/ OTHER COUNTRIES
Aloo	Potatoes
Badaam	Almonds
Baingan	Eggplant, aubergine
Basmati rice	Fragrant Indian rice
Bhutta	Corn
Bhindi	Okra, ladys finger
Capsicum	Bell peppers
Chaawal, Chawal	Rice
Chhoti Illaichi	Green cardamom
Chilli powder	Red chilli powder, Cayenne pepper
Cornflour	Cornstarch
Coriander, fresh	Cilantro
Cream	Heavy whipping cream
Dalchini	Cinnamon
French beans	Green beans
Gajar	Carrots

Gobhi	Cauliflower
Hara Dhania	Cilantro/fresh or green coriander
Hari Gobhi	Broccoli
Hari Mirch	Green hot peppers, green chillies, serrano peppers
Illaichi	Cardamom
Imli	Tamarind
Jeera Powder	Ground cumin seeds
Kadhai/Karahi	Wok
Kaju	Cashewnuts
Katori	Individual serving bowls resembling ramekins
Khumb	Mushrooms
Kishmish	Raisins
Kofta	Balls made from minced vegetables or meat, fried and put in a curry/gravy/sauce.
Maida	All purpose flour, Plain flour
Makai, Makki	Corn
Makhan	Butter
Matar	Peas
Mitha soda	Baking soda
Nimbu	Lemon
Paneer	Home made cheese made by curdling milk with vinegar or lemon juice. Fresh home made ricotta cheese can be substituted.

Patta Gobhi	Cabbage
Phalli	Green beans
Powdered sugar	Castor sugar
Pyaz, pyaaz	Onions
Red Capsicum	Red bell peppers
Red chilli flakes	Red pepper flakes
Saboot Kali mirch	Peppercorns
Saunf	Fennel
Sela Chaawal	Parboiled rice, which when cooked is not sticky at all
Seviyaan	Vermicelli
Shimla Mirch	Green bell peppers
Soda bicarb	Baking soda
Spring Onions	Green onions, Scallions
Suji	Semolina
Tamatar	Tomato
Til	Sesame seeds
Toned Milk	Milk with 1% fat content
Yellow Capsicum	Yellow bell peppers
Zeera	Cumin seeds

INTERNATIONAL CONVERSION GUIDE

These are not exact equivalents; they've been rounded-off to make measuring easier.

WEIGHTS & MEASURES

METRIC	IMPERIAL
15 g	½ oz
30 g	1 oz
60 g	2 oz
90 g	3 oz
125 g	4 oz (¼ lb)
155 g	5 oz
185 g	6 oz
220 g	7 oz
250 g	8 oz (½ lb)
280 g	9 oz
315 g	10 oz
345 g	11 oz
375 g	12 oz (¾ lb)
410 g	13 oz
440 g	14 oz
470 g	15 oz
500 g	16 oz (1 lb)
750 g	24 oz (1½ lb)
1 kg	30 oz (2 lb)

LIQUID MEASURES

METRIC	IMPERIAL
30 ml	1 fluid oz
60 ml	2 fluid oz
100 ml	3 fluid oz
125 ml	4 fluid oz
150 ml	5 fluid oz (¼ pint/1 gill)
190 ml	6 fluid oz
250 ml	8 fluid oz
300 ml	10 fluid oz (½ pint)
500 ml	16 fluid oz
600 ml	20 fluid oz (1 pint)
1000 ml	1¾ pints

CUPS & SPOON MEASURES

METRIC	IMPERIAL
1 ml	¼ tsp
2 ml	½ tsp
5 ml	1 tsp
15 ml	1 tbsp
60 ml	¼ cup
125 ml	½ cup
250 ml	1 cup

HELPFUL MEASURES

METRIC	IMPERIAL
3 mm	1/8 in
6 mm	¼ in
1 cm	½ in
2 cm	¾ in
2.5 cm	1 in
5 cm	2 in
6 cm	2½ in
8 cm	3 in
10 cm	4 in
13 cm	5 in
15 cm	6 in
18 cm	7 in
20 cm	8 in
23 cm	9 in
25 cm	10 in
28 cm	11 in
30 cm	12 in (1ft)

HOW TO MEASURE

When using the graduated metric measuring cups, it is important to shake the dry ingredients loosely into the required cup. Do not tap the cup on the table, or pack the ingredients into the cup unless otherwise directed. Level top of cup with a knife. When using graduated metric measuring spoons, level top of spoon with a knife. When measuring liquids in the jug, place jug on a flat surface, check for accuracy at eye level.

OVEN TEMPERATURE

These oven temperatures are only a guide; lower degree of heat are given. Always check the manufacturer's manual.

	°C (Celsius)	°F (Fahrenheit)	Gas Mark
Very low	120	250	1
Low	150	300	2
Moderately low	160	325	3
Moderate	180	350	4
Moderately high	190	375	5
High	200	400	6
Very high	230	450	7

OTHER TITLES IN THIS SERIES

BEST SELLERS BY

101 Paneer Recipes

101 Vegetarian Recipes

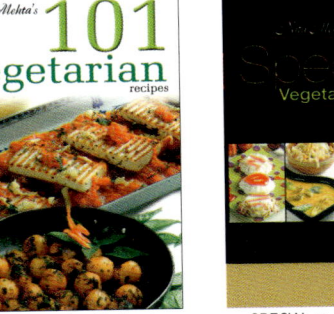

SPECIAL Vegetarian Recipes

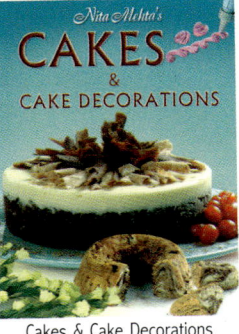

Cakes & Cake Decorations

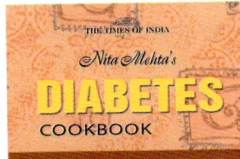

DIABETES Cookbook

Burgers & Sandwiches

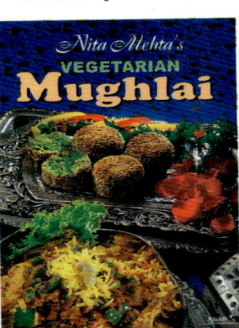

Vegetarian MUGHLAI

CHOCOLATE Cookbook

BEST SELLERS BY

Cooking for Growing Children

Food from Around the World

Great Indian Cooking

Everyday Cooking

Vegetarian Snacks

Vegetarian Chinese

Vegetarian Continental

Zero Oil Cooking